LIVE
MORE
SLOTH

Slow Down, Chill Out and
Live in the Sloth Lane

TIM COLLINS

First published in Great Britain in 2018 by LOM ART, an imprint of
Michael O'Mara Books Limited
9 Lion Yard
Tremadoc Road
London SW4 7NQ

A CIP catalogue record for this book is available from the British Library.

Papers used by Michael O'Mara Books Limited are natural,
recyclable products made from wood grown in sustainable forests.
The manufacturing processes conform to the environmental
regulations of the country of origin.

ISBN: 978-191055-296-4 in hardback print format
ISBN: 978-191055-298-8 in eBook format

1 2 3 4 5 6 7 8 9 10

Designed by Jade Wheaton
Illustrated by Luka Va

Printed and bound by CPI Group (UK) Ltd, Croydon, CR0 4YY

www.mombooks.com

**Thanks to Jo Wyton,
Louise Dixon, Nicki Crossley
and Cinnamon the Sloth.**

CONTENTS

Introduction

I was trekking through the Central American rainforest recently when a strange animal crossed my path. It had long gangly limbs, a small round head and a huge grin.
It was, of course, a sloth.

Three hours later, the creature had finished crossing my path, and I found myself pondering the reason for its broad smile.

I came to the conclusion that the sloth was smiling because it was happy, and the sloth was happy because of the way it lives.

Compare for a moment the sloth and the human.

The human spends its time striving for faster cars, bigger televisions and swankier marble kitchen counters while the sloth desires nothing more than another clawful of leaves.

The human frantically uploads selfies, while the sloth wouldn't bother even if it had opposable thumbs.

The human worries about where it will be in five years' time. The sloth knows exactly where it will be — slightly further along the same branch.

That's when it struck me. If humans could behave more like sloths, they would be happier.

I decided to spend some time living among the sloths and learning from their ways so I could share my findings. Unfortunately, they influenced me so much that I couldn't be bothered taking any notes.

I went back a few months later, remembering to record the details this time. I gathered a panel of expert sloths and asked for their advice about how humans could improve their lives.

I explained many aspects of modern human existence to the creatures and asked what we should be doing differently. It was a long process, partly because they kept falling asleep and partly because it was hard to explain what a telemarketing call was.

I found great wisdom in this strange mammal, and in this book I'll explain how living at the pace of a sloth can lead to greater contentment.

I'll describe how taking time to enjoy nature will enrich your life more than being stuck in a traffic jam in an industrial estate.

I'll describe how single-tasking instead of multitasking can help you slow down to speed up. You can start right now by ditching that sandwich, turning the radio off, leaving the conference call and getting out of the bath.

And I'll describe the fascinating experiments I carried out. For example, I gave a sloth a laptop with the latest version of Excel on and it dropped It oul of a tree. What does this teach us?

Follow the slow path of this creature to a better life. You might even find yourself grinning too.

This book will teach you:

The value of slowing down to sloth pace. Or speeding up to sloth pace, if you're a glacier.

How becoming more sloth can give you the confidence to be yourself. The sloth does not try to be a greyhound. Which is just as well, because even trying to be a pug would be a stretch.

How sloth pace can help you in the rat race.

How you can eat your way to tranquillity with the sloth diet.

Why being a social sloth is better than being a social butterfly.

How adopting the 'downward-facing sloth' — lying on the floor with your arms outstretched — can help you achieve greater happiness. You'll get approached by fewer market researchers, for one thing.

How to become a more slothful parent.

How to sleep soundly and slothfully.

How to rearrange your home so you can live more like a sloth.

The ancient and mysterious art of sloth yoga.

The pastimes that can put you on the path to sloth enlightenment.

How to connect with the natural world like a sloth would.

How to dress more slothfully.

The sloth way to stay calm in the modern world.

How practising slothfulness can give you greater calmness and control.

The Hare, the Tortoise and the Sloth

We've all heard Aesop's fable about the hare and the tortoise. An arrogant mammal races a tortoise, gets overconfident and takes a nap, and the canny reptile wins through its slow, steady progress.

What you might not know is that the first draft of the story was called 'The Hare, the Tortoise and the Sloth'. In it, a sloth looked down from a tree at both animals and wondered why they were bothering to race in the first place. The moral was that dangling from your favourite branch is more enjoyable than giving in to silly competitiveness.

It's a shame Aesop decided to rework his plot, because humanity could have benefitted from this wisdom over the last two thousand years or so. It would have saved us a lot of Olympic Games and performance reviews, for a start.

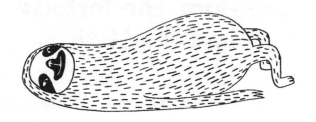

CHAPTER 1

How to Practise
Slothfulness

Slothfulness means calming your busy mind and focusing on the present. It's similar to mindfulness, except that you pretend you're a sloth while you're doing it.

You can practise it anywhere, but the best way is to adopt the 'downward-facing sloth' position by lying on your front with your arms out and your head turned to the side. If anyone in the office asks what you're doing, tell them you'll explain later and then avoid them for ever.

Close your eyes and take deep breaths. Draw your attention to the sound and feeling of your breathing.

If your mind wanders to your to-do list or something annoying your passive-aggressive colleague said, draw it

back to your breathing. Use your breathing to concentrate on the present moment, without thinking about the future or the past.

Think of your mind as a busy rainforest. All your thoughts are noisy animals. That nagging reminder to do your tax return is a howler monkey. The worry that you've left the oven on is a screaming parrot. And the constant background feeling that you haven't got enough work done is the chirping of a hundred Amazon tree crickets.

Imagine all these annoying animals disappearing one by one until you're left with just the tall trees, the thick green leaves and the solitary sloth, hanging from its branch in a state of blissful calm.

Silencing your inner monologue and experiencing true tranquillity takes practice and discipline, but you can achieve it with sloth-like persistence.

Ancient sloths were up to 20 feet long and weighed up to 4 tonnes. They lived in South America from around 50 million years ago to 11,000 years ago. It's a shame they died out because a sloth the size of an elephant would be the coolest pet ever.

CHAPTER 2

Life in the Sloth Lane

It's all so fast these days. We drive fast cars to the fast-food joint before rushing off to the new fast-paced film in the *Fast and Furious* franchise before speeding home for a quick conversation about how terrible it was, then dashing to bed for some rapid eye movement.

You wouldn't catch a sloth doing any of this. With a ground speed of 0.15 miles per hour, the sloth has nothing to fear from a speed camera. Unless there's a harpy eagle perched on it.

Humans put a constant demand on themselves to be busy. At work they accept ever greater levels of responsibility until their calendar becomes a dizzying blur of meetings and deadlines. And going home only plunges them into an urgent list of chores and repairs.

Sloths, on the other hand, have none of this pressure. They feel no guilt about spending a few hours watching clouds drift across the sky. It's pretty much their Netflix.

As you practise slothfulness, you'll learn how to get more out of life by slowing it down.

It means taking time over meals, and becoming aware of the physical acts of chewing and swallowing.

It means slowing down at work, only to find that you get more done.

It means working steadily through your jobs and letting yourself have breaks between each one.

It means approaching activities like walking and reading at a steady pace where you have time to notice small details.

It means not rushing for a train when there's another one just a few minutes later.

It means not tailgating other drivers and flashing your lights just because they're slightly below the speed limit.

Sloths have survived for millions of years because of their slowness. Their main predators rely on spotting movement, so sloths escape their attention and live to enjoy a few more millennia of relaxation.

By slowing down to sloth pace, you can guard against the hazards of modern human life. Just as the sloth escapes eagles, snakes and jaguars, so you can help yourself to avoid stress, anxiety and overload.

It's time to shift your life to 0.15 miles per hour.

CHAPTER 3

Sloth Pace or Rat Race?

Consider the rat-like worker and the sloth-like worker.

Rat wakes up at six, crams itself onto a crowded train, sits through endless meetings, scurries home and collapses on its bed ready to do it all again the next day.

Meanwhile, sloth sets its alarm for seven, but treats itself to a few extra naps and a hot bath before stumbling onto the train so late that it actually gets a seat. Sloth slouches on its chair all day, occasionally tapping on its keyboard, takes the time for a proper lunch break, and slopes off while others are still at work.

Yet sloth manages to get more done than rat. How does that happen?

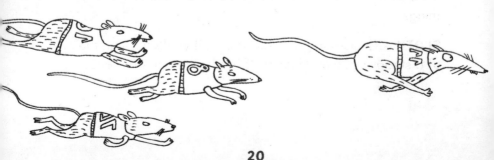

SLOTH FOCUS

RAT flits from task to task, looking busy, but not really achieving much.

SLOTH pauses before everything, making sure it's aware of what it wants to do and how it's going to achieve it.

RAT is a multitasker. It switches between jobs and feels busy, without really getting anything done.

SLOTH is a single-tasker. It continues with a job until it's finished, then moves on to the next thing on its list.

RAT constantly checks emails and breaks away from what it's doing to make phone calls.

SLOTH takes care of these things in chunks so they don't eat up its whole day. Some people get annoyed with sloth for not replying sooner, but sloth doesn't worry about this.

RAT tries to cram more into its day than it can handle. It works late, making small progress on a million different things.

SLOTH sets realistic goals for its day. It works through them at a steady pace and lets itself finish when they're done.

HOW TO BE MORE SLOTH

Be aware of when you're single-tasking and when you're multitasking. Make an achievable list of what you want to do and what order you want to do it in.

Group things like replying to emails and returning phone calls into chunks so they don't dominate your day.

Approach each task with the dedication and focus with which the sloth approaches the tree.

SLOTH SPEED

RAT rushes through its day in a panic. When it faces a tough challenge, it gets stressed and tips over the edge, pacing around the office and yelling into its phone.

SLOTH plods through the day at a measured pace. Even sloth feels stress sometimes, but it energizes rather than overwhelms it.

RAT rushes from one job into the next without pausing for breath.

SLOTH rewards itself with a short break between jobs, enjoying a few moments of rest and silence.

RAT works through lunch, getting blobs of mayonnaise in its keyboard that will prove impossible to clean out. It suffers a massive slump in the middle of the afternoon and gets less done than if it had taken some time off.

SLOTH takes a long break for lunch, seeking out the calmest, greenest space around, even if it's just the patch of grass in the middle of the industrial estate roundabout. It focuses on the act of eating, taking the time to enjoy its food, and returns to work refreshed for a productive afternoon.

HOW TO BE MORE SLOTH

Take a break between each task. You could even go outside and bask in the sun. Or the drizzle. Your ratty colleagues won't think you look busy enough, but as a sloth you won't care.

Put back what you're about to do and take ten minutes to relax. Unless you're a surgeon working in an emergency ward, of course. But the chances are that you can afford to give yourself a little time without anyone actually dying.

Block out a lunch break in your calendar and resist filling it with meetings. Eat slothfully, shutting out distractions and focusing on the act of chewing and swallowing.

SLOTH ATTITUDE

RAT goes to every meeting it's invited to, because rat wants everyone to see how busy it is.

SLOTH avoids meetings it doesn't need to be in and isn't worried about saying 'no'.

RAT talks as much as it can in every meeting, even if it means repeating things that have already been said. Rat thinks about its next job rather than listening to what everyone is saying, and consequently has to wing it when someone asks it what it thinks.

SLOTH takes the time to listen, focusing on the present rather than letting its thoughts drift to what it should do next.

RAT feels like it's getting nothing done, and gets frustrated. It takes it out on the intern rat by yelling at it for bringing a caramel latte rather than a hazelnut one.

SLOTH works steadily through its list of jobs, taking the time to congratulate itself after each one.

RAT wastes energy on office politics that it could be using for work.

SLOTH avoids getting involved in spats. Unless it works with a harpy eagle. Harpy eagles are just horrible.

RAT can't take its mind off the negative aspects of its job. It constantly reminds itself that the boss is an idiot, it doesn't get paid enough and it never gets enough credit for what it does.

SLOTH focuses on the good aspects of its job. It's aware of the things that could be better, but instead of dwelling on them it feels grateful for what's going well.

RAT struggles to switch off when it goes home. It doesn't feel as though it's got enough done, and its mind is on what it needs to do the following day.

SLOTH is happy with the things it has achieved, and manages to enjoy its evening without worrying about work.

HOW TO BE MORE SLOTH

Turn down the meetings you don't really need to attend and concentrate in the ones you do go to. Try to be a good listener, staying fully aware.

Unlike sloths, humans naturally focus on the things that are going wrong. But it's possible to shift your mind out of this habit. Make a conscious effort to think about the things you like about your job, and the things you've done well recently.

When you leave work, try throwing yourself into something that induces a tranquil, slothful state, like reading, painting or walking. Switching to an activity that's different from your job can help you relax quicker.

BE LESS RAT

Most of us would feel a shudder of revulsion if a rat scurried across our path, yet we would be delighted if a sloth ambled past, once we'd stopped wondering what a tropical creature was doing at the bus stop.

Think about how much nicer your company would be if it were full of sloths instead of rats. Be the first sloth and inspire others to join you. You might just turn your workplace into a rainforest of tranquillity.

CHAPTER 4

The Sloth Guide to Hobbies

The sloth doesn't need much in the way of hobbies. It's perfectly happy with its schedule of sleeping, eating and climbing. But if your lifestyle is more stressful, you might need a way to unwind.

The problem is that hobbies can sometimes take so much effort they become just as exhausting as work, and definitely no sloth would approve of that.

I discussed ten different human hobbies with the sloth panel to see which ones got the yawns of approval.

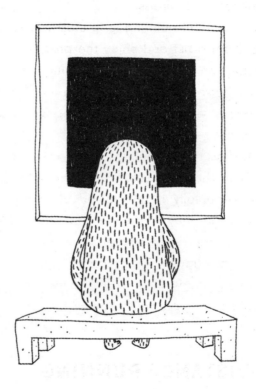

ART

The sloths liked the idea of spending a quiet hour or two with watercolours, and they thought it could be a good way to practise slothfulness.

The key to slothful painting is to stop worrying whether you're a brilliant artist and enjoy the process of creating. Concentrating on your choice of colour and the act of moving your brush over the paper can lull you into calm. Worrying about what your old art teacher would think probably won't.

The sloths had mixed feelings about other forms of art, however. They thought sculpture seemed too much like hard work, especially if it involved chipping marble or beating metal. But they liked conceptual art, especially the sort where you place an everyday object such as a urinal in an art gallery to change our interpretation of it. The sloths were impressed at how little work was involved, and asked if they should enter a partially chewed twig into next year's big art prize.

LONG-DISTANCE RUNNING

The sloths disapproved of this. They don't even run when there's a deadly predator nearby, so it was hard to explain why someone would do it for twenty-six miles when the only thing they're in danger of is missing out on their personal best. They said the runners would be better off staying still and blending into their environment instead, and they should know because they've been around for millions of years.

WALKING

The sloths were much keener on the idea of taking strolls, especially if you can reach the kind of green spaces that resemble their native rainforest. Walking can be a great way to boost your mood and achieve a state of slothfulness.

The sloths especially approved of escaping busy streets and letting the trees and grass calm your thoughts. They love living among greenery, and even turn green themselves in the rainy season, thanks to the algae on their fur.

Their only complaint was that most human walkers go too fast. They recommended keeping to the top sloth speed of 0.15 miles per hour, at which rate you could complete a lap of your local park in just a few days.

GARDENING

Many gardeners get themselves into a state of slothfulness without even intending to. They spend so long working outdoors that they hush their inner monologues and connect with nature.

Gardening involves simple tasks that take you away from glowing screens and all their associated stress. Your thoughts are absorbed in the details of the natural world, and you work yourself into a sloth-like state of calm.

It can also let you enjoy some quiet time, unless your neighbour is in their garden with the radio at full volume. But even if they are, you can learn from sloths. In its natural jungle habitat, the sloth is surrounded by noisy macaws and howler monkeys, but it never lets their din disturb its tranquillity.

The sloths were very impressed with gardening, and gave it their full approval. The only thing that confused them is how gardeners can spend all day around so many delicious twigs and flowers without eating them.

MEDITATION

This got the biggest yawn of approval from the sloths. They naturally spend a lot of time in a meditative state, and they couldn't understand why humans don't do it more. Clearing your head and achieving peace doesn't come as easily to humans as to sloths, but you can get there with practice and patience.

BASE JUMPING

The sloths strongly disapproved of extreme sports such as base jumping, which involves flinging yourself off high buildings or cliffs. One sloth said it accidentally let go of a branch once and doesn't understand why anyone would volunteer for such a frightening experience. Luckily, it landed on the back of an especially soft orang-utan, so no harm was done. It was safely back on its branch just a few hours later and was able to put the whole experience behind it.

READING

The sloths definitely approved of this, especially if it involves sitting on a comfy chair while wearing a sleeved blanket and staying still for hours on end.

Reading is such a big part of our lives, from newspapers to text messages to humblebragging status updates, that it's easy to take for granted. But reading for a long time can lull you into calmness, especially if you approach it in a slothful way.

If you spend a lot of time reading on screens, it's worth switching to physical books when you're at home. One of the many great things about actual books is that they don't have the Instagram app on them, so you won't get distracted by how great a time your friend is having in Cuba.

A slothful reader will go through text slowly and carefully, savouring the pieces of description that evoke a person or a place. Books can appeal to all your senses, engaging your imagination and absorbing you fully. You can lull yourself into a meditative state just by wanting to find out what happens next.

However, the sloths made the good point that anyone reading this will already know all about books, so I don't need to bang on about it.

WRITING

There are hundreds of different types of writing, and any of them could help to focus and calm your mind. Except for getting drunk and writing a long email to your ex. That one probably won't.

You could try anything from writing down your stream of thoughts to penning an erotic vampire novel in which the main character looks suspiciously like you.

As with painting, you should switch off inner critical thoughts about whether you're doing it properly and focus on the act itself as a way to clear your mind.

The sloths approved of this hobby too, especially if you can do it by sitting still and scribbling quietly rather than pacing around the room and grimacing as you search for the perfect metaphor.

KNITTING

The sloths were also keen on this one. They said that concentrating on the simple, repetitive nature of the task could inspire a state of slothfulness. They even considered having a go themselves, using their long claws as knitting needles, but decided to sleep instead.

BIRDWATCHING

As another hobby that involves sitting still and being quiet, I thought this might get a yawn of approval from the sloths. But they only looked around with worried expressions on their faces when I mentioned it. Whoops! I should have remembered that eagles are among the sloth's main predators, so looking out for birds is one of the few things they do that isn't relaxing.

CHAPTER 5

Eat Like a Sloth

Dining is something we all do every day, unless we're supermodels. It's a simple act we take for granted, yet it can be turned into a useful slothfulness exercise if you give it your full attention.

You can focus on the act of eating just like you'd focus on inhaling and exhaling in a breathing exercise. You should find that you emerge from your lunchbreak with a sense of deep inner calm. Unless the thing you ate on your lunch break was chicken vindaloo.

HOW TO EAT SLOTHFULLY

For many modern humans, meals have become another thing to cross off the to-do list. Lunch is a wilting sandwich at the desk and dinner is a soggy wrap on the train home. Even a meal out is marred by the stress of trying to get the waiter's attention without looking like an impatient idiot.

Now consider the sloth as it inches from tree to tree, savouring the taste of every leaf. The creature takes the time to enjoy each mouthful, focusing on the simple act of eating.

Be as slow and deliberate as a sloth as you choose your meal. Linger over the options, unless you're in Subway and there's a massive queue behind you.

When you get your food, take a moment before starting it, becoming aware of the feeling of hunger in your stomach and the watering in your mouth.

When you take your first bite, chew slowly. This will give you a deeper appreciation of the texture and flavour of your food, so make sure you don't do it if you've just bought something from the dining car on a train.

No mammal digests as slowly as the sloth. Pay tribute to it by leaving gaps between each mouthful and being aware of your own digestion. This could stop you accidentally overeating. The sloth might not have much of a six pack, but it knows when to quit scoffing and move on to other important activities such as dangling from branches.

If you still find yourself scarfing it down, develop a ritual such as putting your fork on the table between each bite. The slower you can make yourself go, the more chance you'll give your stomach to signal to your brain that it's full.

Another useful ritual can be to only ever eat at a dining table or in the kitchen. Eating from your lap in front of the TV is a sure-fire way to distract yourself from the messages your body is sending and overeat.

Sticking to clear eating routines is also helpful. Planning meals in advance could be useful, especially if it means you always have enough food in the house and don't go scrabbling around in that drawer for the takeaway menus.

Being more aware of your stomach's signals can also help you eat only when your body is telling you that it's hungry, rather than because you're bored or because there was a great deal on chocolate by the checkout at the supermarket.

Take a few moments of calm and silence when you've finished your slothful eating. Stay aware of your digestion and the feelings in your stomach before moving on, and make this leisurely pace part of your routine.

THE SLOTH DIET

The sloth can inspire your choice of food as well as the pace of your eating. The diet of the sloth is made up mostly of leaves, so let the sloth guide you and ignore the Turkey Twizzlers in your freezer in favour of the salad in your fridge.

As well as leaves, sloths eat insects and rodents. Admittedly, the sloth diet plan falls down here. Eating live caterpillars would certainly focus your attention on eating, as well as the attention of everyone around you and the millions who would eventually end up watching the footage on YouTube.

So let's just substitute nuts, meat or cheese for these things. But by all means think of them as mice if it helps you pretend you're a sloth.

Sloths aren't big drinkers, which is just as well as they only go to the toilet once a week. But they get a lot of water from their leaves, so make sure you drink plenty too.

As you might expect, the simple act of drinking a glass of water is a great anchor for practising slothfulness. As with food, a slow pace is the key to unlocking slothful tranquillity.

It's a lot like the slothful breathing exercise described at the start of this book, except you won't get far if you try it lying face-down. Sit down with a glass of water and take a few moments to focus. Take a sip, concentrating on the sensation of the liquid washing through your mouth.

Take the time to stop and breathe between sips, placing the glass on a table if it helps to slow things down. Repeat this over and over again until you clear your mind of thoughts about the past and the future and are focused fully on the present.

And yes, before you ask, the same exercise would work with wine or beer. But the danger is that you'll enjoy it so much you'll do it over and over again and the next morning you'll have no choice but to stay in bed in the sloth position.

CHAPTER 6

The Social Sloth

Sloths aren't social creatures by nature. They don't dislike company, but they're perfectly happy without it.

If you're an outgoing, gregarious person and you like to be around people all the time, great. But there's a lot of pressure these days to pretend to be like this even if you aren't.

It might be time to stop trying to become a social butterfly and let yourself be a social sloth.

SOCIAL BUTTERFLY OR SOCIAL SLOTH?

BUTTERFLY spends all its time with others, even when it makes it feel exhausted.

SLOTH sets aside time to spend alone and sticks to it.

BUTTERFLY feels like it should make small talk whenever it's around people, even if this makes it feel awkward.

SLOTH is happy to remain quiet in company.

BUTTERFLY forces itself to network, even when it feels uncomfortable.

SLOTH doesn't put pressure on itself to meet everyone in the room who could help its career.

BUTTERFLY accepts every social invitation, until its time off becomes more exhausting than its job.

SLOTH isn't afraid of turning things down. If it sets time aside to practise slothfulness, it sticks to it, even if it means saying 'no' to a social engagement.

BUTTERFLY goes out every night.

SLOTH enjoys solitary hobbies like reading, painting and walking.

BUTTERFLY feels drained.

SLOTH feels fresh.

SLOTHFULNESS FOR INTROVERTS

You might think that you're naturally a social sloth if you enjoy spending time alone, and already take regular breaks from socializing. But there's more to true slothfulness than this.

The person sitting silently on their own might look perfectly relaxed. But introverts tend to be internally noisy even if they're outwardly quiet.

They can have an inner monologue running, reminding them of their current worries and obsessions. Escaping these busy thoughts is the goal of slothfulness, and it can be especially tough for introverts.

Learning to calm your noisy mind takes patience, as you fixate on breathing or sipping a glass of water over and over again. But like a sloth climbing an especially tall and slippery tree with determination, you'll get there in the end.

SLOTHFULNESS FOR EXTROVERTS

If you're an extrovert, you might face a different set of problems as you approach slothfulness. Blocking out time to spend on your own might feel unnatural, especially if it means rejecting a social engagement.

Being still for long periods without external stimuli will feel very strange at first, and it may take a while to get over your feelings of awkwardness. Keeping your attention on something as simple as breathing may seem strange when you're used to constant social interaction, and you might feel like giving up. But stick with slothfulness and you could find these periods of calm give your life more balance.

Even if you're a butterfly and proud, transforming into a sloth every now and then has its uses.

THE BENEFITS OF SLOTHFULNESS

As well as giving you moments of peace, slothfulness can also help when you return to the social world.

Slothfulness helps you focus more fully on the present, making you a better listener. No longer will you be waiting for a pause in your friend's monologue so you can share what's on your mind. You'll be engaging fully with what they're saying and asking relevant questions.

And if you can tap into the calm you feel in slothful moments, it might help you get through stressful social situations. For example, next time a loud work colleague repeats the point you've just made and gets the credit for it, imagine you're peacefully swinging from a branch in the rainforest. This should prevent you from pressing a sandwich into their face and yelling, 'That was my idea!'

As you continue your journey into slothfulness, your greater relaxation could help you project greater social confidence. Everyone in the rainforest wants to be sloth's friend, because sloth isn't desperate to be friends with them. Marmosets, okapi and toucans all exaggerate how close they are to sloth, even though it feels pretty indifferent about them.

SOCIAL MEDIA FOR SOCIAL SLOTHS

The social-media phenomenon hasn't affected sloths yet. Very few of them have Facebook, Twitter or Instagram accounts and as far as we know none of them has ever taken a selfie, though their long arms would save them money on selfie sticks.

As a result, sloths have never had to deal with the pressure that comes from looking at the profiles of social butterflies.

Many humans feel jealous or anxious when viewing the updates of others. Of course, you're comparing your mundane moments to someone else's highlight reel, so it's never going to be fair. But even if you keep this in mind, social media has a way of getting under your fur.

If you're suffering from this, the best thing to do might be to stay away. Spend the time you would have spent scanning humblebrag updates with a good book instead. Or delete the apps from your phone and google sloth pictures instead.

But if this seems too drastic, you could just approach social media in a sloth-like way.

Sloth would never waste energy feeling jealous of the exclusive beach resort your friend is staying in. It's never found a cocktail as tasty as the average leaf or a four-poster as comfortable as the average branch.

Scroll through social media slowly, and observe how it affects you. Our minds constantly tell us stories about ourselves, and we fit the information we receive into them. One day we might tell ourselves that we're not as rich and exciting as certain friends; the next we might be glad we're not as boastful as them.

It would be great to approach your social-media feed in a sloth-like state of calm in which you aren't judging anyone, but that isn't always possible. Some people make it really hard not to mutter judgemental labels under your breath. But at least staying aware of how your mind is interpreting the incessant grumbling or vainglorious happiness of your friends can lead to a calmer experience.

The mysteries of social-media algorithms mean that sometimes you get a hundred likes for a picture of a smoothie and other times you get just three for your newborn child. It doesn't mean your smoothie is especially attractive and your child isn't, it just means that sometimes people see what you post and sometimes they don't.

Remember that no sloth would care if you clicked on a 'thumbs-up' button or not. They don't even have thumbs, so it would mean nothing to them.

CHAPTER 7

The Sloth Guide to Holidays

In theory, a week away should be the ideal time to escape our busy lives and lounge around like a sloth. But in practice, holidays can be just as hectic as the lives we're getting away from. We make a to-do list of places we want to see and things we want to do, and we're on the flight home before we're even halfway through it, haunted by a sense that we didn't make the most of it.

I described ten types of human holiday to the sloth panel to get their thoughts.

LOUNGING BY THE POOL

The sloths approved of this one. They are surprisingly good swimmers, so they liked the idea of taking a dip in the pool, and they thought spending the rest of the time reading and eating sounded pretty good too.

They suggested practising slothfulness by taking time to observe the small details of your new surroundings. Listen to the sploshing of the water, feel the heat on your skin and take a deep breath of the air. You can even adopt the downward-facing sloth position on your lounger and it won't look odd.

CAMPING

The sloths loved the idea of spending time immersed in nature, especially if you live in a city. They thought that a week in a calming green space could easily bring on a state of slothfulness. They also mentioned that if you're worried about the toilet facilities in the great outdoors, you should take a leaf from their book and hold it in for a week.

SIGHTSEEING

The sloths weren't so sure about this. Nice as it might be to view famous landmarks through your own eyes, or at least through your own phone screen, the sloths thought this had the potential to become the sort of holiday that isn't really much of a break at all.

Sloths don't like cities, even if they're famous ones with lots of expensive restaurants and old churches, rather than boring ones with lots of industrial estates and pound shops. And they couldn't understand why anyone would choose to go to one when they could be dangling from a branch instead.

But the sloths suggested that sightseers should at least build time for relaxing into their schedules. They also warned against photographing absolutely everything, chronicling your trip on social media and constantly refreshing your apps to see who approves. They suggested that taking quiet moments to fix your attention on the details of your new environments might help you achieve inner calm, even if the world around you remains a mad bustle.

CRUISE SHIPS

Sloths love water, so they were initially keen on this option, but they went off it when I mentioned that the ships can travel as fast as thirty miles an hour. They didn't think anything that happens at such a reckless pace could ever count as a holiday.

CLUBBING

Sloths like nothing more than sleep, so the idea of going without any for a week and counting it as a holiday was incomprehensible to them. And they only got even more confused when I showed them some footage of a nightclub. They asked if the constant whooping was the human equivalent of the high-pitched sloth mating call, and I said they were more or less right.

BACKPACKING

The sloths said they approved of any holidaymakers who put happiness above basic personal hygiene. But they didn't like the ambitious itineraries backpackers attempt. They thought backpackers should slow down to sloth speed and spend their gap year crawling to the local shops and back.

ROCK FESTIVALS

The sloths said that spending a weekend in mud surrounded by loud screaming didn't sound very relaxing, but they'd mention it to the howler monkeys as it sounded like their sort of thing.

ACTIVITY HOLIDAYS

The sloths thought this would be a good idea if the activities in question were sleeping and letting moths nest on you. But they were confused to hear that anyone would count white-water rafting as suitable behaviour on holiday.

A TREK THROUGH THE SOUTH AMERICAN RAINFOREST

At first the sloths thought this was a wonderful idea. Their grins widened as they described all the brilliant trees holidaymakers could see. But then they realized that the last thing they wanted was tourists stomping around and disturbing their peace, so they quickly backpedalled and pointed out that rainforests are full of poison dart frogs, bullet ants and green anacondas, and any humans who venture in will almost certainly die.

CHAPTER 8

Sloth Yoga

The sloth spends most of its waking hours in a state of tranquil bliss with its body in strange shapes, so it pretty much does yoga all the time. Add these sloth-inspired poses to your programme and set yourself on the path to tranquillity.

SAFETY NOTE: All of these sloth positions have been verified as suitable for humans, but that does not mean you should attempt to replicate everything you see the sloth do. Three-toed sloths have extra vertebrae in their necks, allowing them to swivel their heads through 270 degrees. If you attempt this you could end up in the emergency room with a lot of explaining to do.

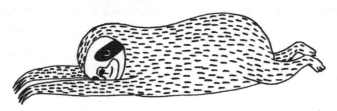

POSITION ONE
The Downward-facing Sloth

This is the classic sloth position, and it simply involves slumping down on the ground with your head to the side and your arms outstretched as if you were crawling at 0.15 miles per hour. Unlike the classic 'downward-facing dog' position, it doesn't involve any difficult stretching. You just have to flop down onto the floor.

POSITION TWO
The Downward-facing Sloth on an exercise ball

If you have an inflatable exercise ball, you should incorporate it into your routine as a sloth would. Try to sit on it for a while, but then give up and collapse back into the traditional sloth position for a nap.

POSITION THREE

The Hanging Sloth

Sloths love hanging upside down. They eat, sleep and mate like this, and their internal organs have even evolved so there isn't too much weight on their diaphragms in this position, so that breathing is easy.

Pay tribute to this amazing skill by curling into a ball and grasping an imaginary branch. Try not to spend so long in this position that your internal organs adapt to it too. Staying fixed like this for ten deep breaths should be enough.

POSITION FOUR

The Upward-grasping Sloth

Sloths bend themselves into some odd shapes as they grasp up at high branches for tasty leaves. In this position, you keep one of your feet and one of your hands on the floor, stick your other foot out at a ninety-degree angle, and grasp as high as you can with your other hand. It's not easy to sustain, but try to hold it for ten breaths.

POSITION FIVE

The Forward Collapse

Forward bends are a very important part of regular yoga, and they feature in sloth yoga too. To get into position, you have to pretend you're a sloth who's reached up for a high branch but fallen asleep halfway through. It will be much less comfortable for a human than a sloth, but you should be able to hold it for ten breaths.

POSITION SIX

The Backward Collapse

To achieve this position, you should imagine you're a sloth with its lower legs dangling over the edge of a branch who's fallen asleep and collapsed back onto a lower branch. As you don't have a branch, you'll have to lie on the floor and lift your knees and back into the classic yoga 'cat' position. Again, it will be harder for you to hold than a sloth, so you can release yourself after ten breaths.

POSITION SEVEN

The Dangling Sloth

Sometimes sloths show off by dangling upside down from branches using just the claws on their hind feet. Although you probably don't have long enough toenails to do the same, you can pay tribute with a headstand. This is quite an advanced yoga move, and you might need a wall for support, but it's worth mastering if you really want to act and think like the sloth.

POSITION EIGHT

The Crumpled Lotus

Perhaps the most iconic yoga pose of all, the lotus position involves sitting cross-legged with your feet placed on their opposing thighs. It's said that the position is so stable that you can drift off to sleep without falling over. The sloth yoga version of the pose is much easier to achieve. You simply have to start pulling your feet into position before giving up and collapsing backwards.

Stop worrying about the future.
The sloth does not care what will happen
next Wednesday. It doesn't even know what
a Wednesday is. All it knows is the present
moment, whether it's swimming, relaxing on
a branch or pretending to be a coconut so
a harpy eagle doesn't spot it.

CHAPTER 9

The Art of
Sloth Confidence

One of the most inspiring things about sloths is how happy they are in their own fur. They hang around on branches all day, grinning at the world.

Unlike some animals, they don't seek constant validation. You don't need to pat them on the head and tell them they're a clover boy, and if you tried to make them perform on an agility course at Crufts, they'd simply yawn and go to sleep.

Sloths don't care if a passing howler monkey shouts abuse at them. They just shrug and get on with their day.

Sloths are the perfect model of self-confidence. Humans, on the other hand, often struggle. Some of them are raised with the mistaken belief that being hard on themselves is good, and they go through life with a negative internal commentary.

However, all this can be overcome with the guidance of the sloth.

PUT YOURSELF INTO A SLOTHFUL STATE

If you're experiencing self-critical thoughts, try getting into a sloth-like state by focusing on a simple act like breathing or sipping a glass of water.

As well as letting you have a break from your thoughts, a slothfulness exercise can give you a different perspective on them. You'll be aware that they're just thoughts, which might be right and might be wrong.

Thoughts run through our minds all the time, and many of them turn out to be untrue. I used to think that the song 'Livin' on a Prayer' contained the line, 'It doesn't make a difference if we're naked or not', for example.

You could replace 'I won't succeed at this task' with 'I'm thinking that I won't succeed at this task'. This awareness of negative thoughts and how they affect you can be an important step towards changing them.

STAY ON THE LOOKOUT FOR NEGATIVE THOUGHTS

Just as the sloth must watch out for eagles, snakes and jaguars, so you should watch out for negative thoughts. Observe them as they approach and recognize the threat they pose. As you develop a keen eye for incoming self-criticism, you might come to question the negative assumptions you've been taking for granted.

THINK ABOUT WHAT YOU'RE DOING WELL

Try to drown out criticism by focusing on positive things about yourself. These don't have to be anything major. For example, the sloth just has to think about how good it is at hanging onto branches without falling off and it feels good.

AVOID UNHELPFUL COMPARISONS

One of the ways we deplete our self-esteem is by constantly comparing ourselves to people we think are doing better. This can be an ingrained habit that makes it hard to focus on the good things about ourselves.

Again, the sloth can be a great inspiration here. It doesn't worry about its rainforest neighbours. It knows it will always be the best at hanging from branches and waiting a week to go to the toilet, and that's enough for it to feel good.

ADOPT THE SLOTH POSTURE

Some people will advise you that standing up straight with your shoulders back and your chest thrust out projects self-confidence. But if you've tried this and it made you feel weird, try the sloth posture instead. Hunch your shoulders, drag your feet across the floor, turn your head to the side and eat a flower. This posture also projects self-confidence. After all, no one who walks around like this can be too worried about what anyone else thinks.

SMILE LIKE A SLOTH

It's said that your facial expression can influence your mood, as well as the way other people react to you. So why not fix the serene smile of the sloth on your face? You'll project the inner calm of one of the planet's most contented creatures.

PRETEND YOU'RE A SLOTH

Some people find it helpful to visualize a more confident version of themselves when they're in a high-pressure situation such as a meeting or interview. So imagine yourself clinging to a branch in a rainforest and see if it helps you to project sloth confidence.

Set aside time to disconnect from the digital world. Switch off your phone, laptop, tablet and TV and enjoy sloth-like simplicity. Just don't announce you're about to do it on Facebook and spend the whole time wondering if anyone commented.

CHAPTER 10

The Sloth Transport Guide

Getting from one point to another isn't very stressful for a sloth. They spot a good tree, find a vine that will get them there, and arrive safely a few hours later. Or a few days later, if they're not feeling rushed.

Humans, on the other hand, don't have it so easy. They seem to have designed the process of moving between places to be as annoying as possible. Here are a few sloth tips for staying calm on transport, however difficult that might be.

PLANES

All flying things remind the sloths of their enemy the harpy eagle, so they took an instant dislike to planes. Their hostility only grew when I explained that planes moved at 4,000 times the speed of a sloth.

But perhaps flying isn't such a bad option for slothfulness. If you arrive at the airport with plenty of time to spare, the endless queuing won't seem so stressful and you'll have time for a few relaxation exercises when you get there.

Adopting the downward-facing sloth position probably won't go down too well in an environment where security guards are on the lookout for suspicious behaviour, but you should be able to find somewhere to sit and focus on your breathing.

Achieving slothful tranquillity on the plane itself will be harder. Between the screaming baby behind you, the territorial battle for the armrest with the person next to you, and the man in front who's leant his seat so far back his dandruff is sprinkling onto your latte, just getting through the flight without erupting into air rage can feel like a big achievement.

Things are unlikely to get more comfortable any time soon, as the average human continues to get bigger and seats continue to shrink so airlines can offer lower prices.

But sloth tranquillity can be achieved if you work at it.

TRAINS AND SUBWAYS

I explained modern systems of trains and subways to the sloths, but they couldn't understand why humans would put themselves through anything so upsetting. Even the benign sloth would emerge from a packed rush-hour train snarling like a Dobermann, so it's just as well they'll never have to experience them.

The tricky thing is to channel the calm and wisdom of the sloth while you're on a train, even though you know that none of them would be stupid enough to ever get on one. A simple slothfulness exercise might help, but that's not easy when you can't even get a seat, let alone lie face-down on the floor.

Also, slothfulness is all about focusing your attention on the present, but if you did that on a packed train rather than counting down the minutes until you could escape, you'd go mad.

There was one aspect of modern trains that the sloth approved of, however. It was very keen on the buses put on when work's being done on the train track, which have the exact same ground speed as an especially lazy sloth.

DRIVING

The sloths were predictably scornful about cars, especially when I described how humans are so obsessed with making them go fast that they need speed limits, cameras, speed bumps and road narrowing. And still most drivers act like they've just been given three mushrooms in *Mario Kart*.

As we all know, overtaking drivers who are going at the speed limit won't achieve anything, except giving them a good laugh when you both get stuck at the next lights. But driving too slowly can also be dangerous, so it might seem that the car isn't the best place to practise slothfulness.

And yet there few times when we need sloth-like peace more than when we're behind the wheel. Whether it's an unexpected jam, someone stealing your parking space or the sheer audacity of the phrase 'traffic calming', driving seems to have been designed to send your blood pressure rocketing.

But it's possible to practise slothfulness while driving. Take the long, scenic route, where you'll be surrounded by green spaces. Drive a little below the limit if there's no one behind to beep you. And turn the radio off and focus fully on the present.

CYCLING

I showed the sloths a picture of a bike and they said they wouldn't go on one even if their limbs were more powerful than pipe-cleaners.

There might have been a time when cycling in a slothful frame of mind would have been possible. But it would have been back when bikes were still known as 'pushbikes' and they were used mainly for cycling down country lanes to church. These days you've got to keep pace with drivers or suffer their aggressive beeping and shouting. Or you could brave the pavements and try to swerve around oblivious pedestrians with their eyes on their phone screens.

As a means of getting around a busy city, cycling is unlikely to ever help you relax. But find a rural cycle path and it's a different story. You'll be able to go at a leisurely pace, white vans won't cut you up, and the open green spaces will make sloth-like tranquillity easy to achieve.

WALKING

The sloths approved of this option. While bipedalism hasn't been known in their world since the days of their flashy ancestor the giant ground sloth, it's no problem for most humans.

Obviously, walking won't always be an option. But you might find that some journeys are more walkable than you've assumed. Don't be like those tourists in London who spend twenty minutes getting from Piccadilly Circus to Leicester Square by Tube.

You can use walking as a slothfulness exercise to switch your focus to the present and stop worrying about the past and the future. Green spaces such as parks will make this easier, but you could manage it anywhere.

Slothful walking works better at a slow pace, so cut down a side street if you think you'll be holding up angry people. Focus your attention on the physical sensations of walking, like your breathing and the weight of your feet pushing into the ground. Use these as an anchor, and come back to them if your attention wanders.

Dropping your gaze slightly might help you concentrate on the act of walking, but make sure you still have enough awareness of your surroundings that you don't get flattened by a cyclist.

By making time in your day for a slothful walk, you can arrive at your destination in a tranquil state. The sloths suggested walking whenever possible, and only using other types of transport when you absolutely have to.

CHAPTER 11

The Natural Sloth

There's a reason why sloths never chopped down their rainforest, concreted it over and opened a fast-food restaurant selling deep-fried flowers and twigs. The sloth knows that it's easier to feel peaceful when it's surrounded by nature.

Much of the sloth's calmness comes from the connection to nature it gets from literally hugging trees. Is the sloth a hippy? Of course. Its fur is so long and unkempt that algae grows on it. The only way it could be more of a hippy is if it spontaneously developed tie-dye markings.

Adopting the sloth's attitude to green spaces can help you achieve a greater sense of inner calm, especially if you're the sort of person whose main experience of the natural world comes from accidentally looking at window boxes.

If you spend your life surrounded by concrete, glass, metal and plastic, you've pretty much turned yourself into a zoo animal. But unlike other zoo animals, you can escape your cage without ending up on the news. Put time aside for a rural excursion and follow these sloth tips for getting the most out of it.

BREATHE

Breathing exercises are one of the simplest ways of getting yourself into a state of sloth-like tranquillity. And where better to do them than in green spaces? It's much nicer to fix your attention on your breathing when you can smell wild flowers rather than the bins outside the kebab shop.

LISTEN

The sounds of nature can be a great anchor for your attention as you lull yourself into slothfulness. Listen to the wind in the leaves, the gentle crashing of waves and the distant cries of birds. The sloth consultants also recommended listening out for jaguars, but that probably won't be a problem in your average park.

TOUCH

Pick up an object like a pebble or a leaf and focus on the sensation of touching it. Use it as an anchor to fix your mind on the present, constantly drawing your attention back to it.

The sloth connects to nature through all its senses, and you should smell it, listen to it and touch it as well as looking at it. You can even taste it if you like. Just stay away from those funny mushrooms unless you want to be found slumped at the side of the road four hours later, gibbering about how we're all part of the cosmic consciousness.

GO SOMEWHERE NEW

Visit a beach, hill or forest you've never been to before. Going somewhere different can make it easier to lose yourself in your surroundings and achieve sloth-like peace.

SIT STILL

Find a quiet spot where you can sit undisturbed for a few minutes. Concentrate on the things in front of you, whether they're gently collapsing waves, swaying trees or the shifting light on a meadow. It's much easier to calm your mind in natural settings, so they're great places for slothfulness. This is why sloths always smile, while urban foxes do nothing but scowl.

So much of the stress we're trying to escape comes from the incessant schedules of urban living. The working hours, the transport timetables, the endless things we were meant to do yesterday and the million things we want to do tomorrow.

Nature moves at its own pace, and sometimes sitting in it and observing it can help you escape yours.

WALK

As well as sitting still, walking can be a great way to let the tranquillity of the natural world into your mind. And unlike walking in a busy city, you can go as slowly as you like without anyone shoving you aside as they hurry to a meeting.

Pick out small details and focus on them as you go. It might help to stop and concentrate on something like a tree or plant for a few minutes before moving on. As with slothful walking in a city, you can also settle your attention on the feelings of walking. Feel your feet pressing against the inside of your boots and your boots pushing into the ground.

COLLECT

Take your mind off your to-do list by setting yourself a simple collecting task. You could choose shells, pine cones or you could pay tribute to the sloth by looking for delicious leaves and twigs. Collecting can be a good way to fix your attention on the world around you and achieve a state of slothfulness.

IGNORE DIGITAL DISTRACTIONS

Take out your earbuds, close your email app and put your phone away. Probably best to keep it with you in case you get trapped by the incoming tide or something, but setting aside your gadgets can help you focus on your environment.

And if you do achieve a state of perfect calm, try not to post about it on Facebook, then immediately worry that you didn't get enough likes.

CLIMB A TREE

Seeing nature as the sloth does can help you achieve a more tranquil state. So why not climb a tree and dangle from a branch while eating leaves? At least if you do this in the middle of the countryside you've got less chance of being spotted and ending up on YouTube.

Sloths go so long without baths or haircuts
that their fur houses moths and algae.
The algae have a symbiotic relationship
with the sloth, turning it green during
the rainy season and camouflaging
it. It's probably not a great idea to
imitate this, but you might at least get
an entire train carriage to yourself.

CHAPTER 12

The Slothful Home

If you really want to live like a sloth, nothing beats a tree. Sell your home, move to the jungle and build yourself a luxury treehouse complete with bathroom, kitchen and bedrooms.

    If this is not a realistic option, or if you just don't fancy the commute from central America, there are still a number of ways you can bring slothfulness into your home.

PLANNING YOUR SLOTH SPACE

The sloth's home consists of nothing but the branch they're dangling from, and decluttering can bring you closer to its simple existence. A comfortable bed and sofa are needed for relaxing, but avoid overloading your house with other items of furniture. Choose tables and bedside cabinets with drawers, so items can be easily cleared away. A sparse living space can help you achieve a calmer state of mind.

Indoor plants can be a good way to evoke the sloth's natural environment. And if you're choosing wall colours, go for the sorts of relaxing greens and browns that the sloth would find in its home. The trick is to evoke the sloth's habitat without actually recreating it. There would be nothing relaxing about whacking the heating up and filling your living room with jaguars.

SKIP CHORES

It's great to get on top of the housework, but if you're spending every moment at home in the middle of some lengthy chore, it might be time to rethink. You wouldn't catch a sloth scrubbing its branch with a pair of rubber gloves on.

The most obvious tip here follows on from the previous one. If you keep your possessions to a minimum, it will be less work to look after them. If you're spending your whole life separating your clothes into differently coloured piles for washing, you might own too many clothes. At the very least, consider becoming a goth so you only ever have to do a dark wash.

By the same token, other aspects of sloth living will help you cut down on household jobs. A sloth-inspired salad won't take five pans to cook, and quiet nights in will require less ironing than a hectic social life.

Set aside a certain amount of time for cleaning and don't go over it. There are always more surfaces that could be dusted and wiped. Give priority to the most essential tasks and skip the rest so you can spend longer in a state of sloth-like relaxation.

TURN HOUSEWORK INTO SLOTHFULNESS EXERCISES

On the other hand, sloth-like doesn't have to mean slob-like. While it's good to cut out inessential chores, there are a few that you'll need to tackle if you want your home to stay relaxing. It's great to adopt the downward-facing sloth position on purpose, but not if you tripped over last night's plate while trying to make your way across the living room.

The trick with these unavoidable chores is to turn them into slothfulness exercises. You can use a simple act like washing up or cleaning a floor to fix your mind on the present and tune out thoughts about the past or the future.

Work slowly, giving the household job your full attention, and immersing yourself in the mundane details. Notice the thoughts that drift through your mind, but return your focus to the task.

Getting through essential chores and achieving slothfulness at the same time is a handy trick if you can master it. Your mind will already be in a state of calm as you leave your chores behind and move on to your leisure time.

BATHE SLOTHFULLY

Sloths have no sweat glands, so they can ignore personal hygiene in a way that humans can't. There's no point in achieving sloth-like levels of tranquillity if everyone around you is driven into a rage by your pong.

Fortunately, washing can be very relaxing, so there's no need to skip it. Try soaking in a deep tub surrounded by scented candles rather than grabbing a shower while worrying about a meeting. Take your time over the washing ritual, using it to separate your hectic working day from your slothful home time.

Many aspects of personal hygiene can be turned into slothfulness exercises. For example, you might brush your teeth in an early morning daze, but the act can be used to fix your mind on the present. Concentrate on the feeling of the brush against your teeth and the taste of the toothpaste. Bring yourself back to the simple, repetitive motion of the act every time your mind drifts.

Slothful brushing can help you start your day in a calm frame of mind, and it will also mean you'll have spotless teeth when the time comes to flash your sloth-like smile.

THROW AWAY YOUR TV

Remember when TV used to be relaxing? We'd switch it on after work, watch half a detective show and nod off. These days we need to subscribe to fifteen different streaming services, and we spend all our time browsing through endless menus for something we're in the mood for.

When we finally pick something, the buffering issues begin, leaving us staring at a percentage in the middle of a spinning circle.

There are hundreds of shows our friends insist we watch, all of which have five seasons that last eighteen hours each. As a result, watching TV has become another stressful chore to add to our growing to-do list.

As ever, the sloth has the answer. It doesn't know what happened on *The Walking Dead* last night, and it has no idea what a *Game of Thrones* is. That's because it watches clouds instead of TV. So why not follow its lead? Ditch the telly and look at the sky in all its 3D, widescreen, 4K glory.

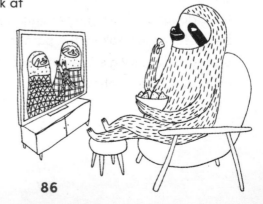

GET A SLOTHFUL PET

While it's illegal to get an actual sloth, there are few substitutes you might want to consider. Rabbits, hamsters and guinea pigs are cute, fairly low maintenance and spend a lot of time sleeping, but they don't quite give off the same relaxing vibes as the sloth.

Dogs should probably be avoided, as they need regular walking and are incredibly needy, making them terrible role models for slothful living. If you insist on getting one, pugs are an option as they're fairly lethargic, but even they're a hassle.

Perhaps the best thing to go for would be an especially lazy cat. If you get one with long, unkempt fur, it could almost pass for a sloth as it lounges about in a patch of sunlight.

If only a sloth will do, however, you could always adopt one. A number of animal charities and zoos will send you a photo of a sloth and a certificate of adoption in exchange for a donation. Having a specific creature to focus on can be useful as you follow the path to slothful enlightenment, and you'll be giving something back to the species that has offered you so much wisdom.

CHAPTER 13

The Sloth Guide to Sleeping

Sloths in captivity can sleep for over sixteen hours a day, which is one of the reasons they got a reputation as the world's most lethargic animal. However, recent research has found that they don't sleep quite as much in the wild. Sloths in the rainforest of Panama were fitted with sleep-monitoring devices in 2008. It was found that they actually sleep around ten hours a day, about the same as a human infant or student.

This is pretty unremarkable as far as the animal kingdom goes. It's much less than the eighteen hours lazy armadillos need, but a lot more than the two hours elephants get. I suppose it must be hard to switch off and get some kip when you can't stop remembering things.

So while the sloth isn't quite the lie-in king, it seems to know a thing or two about getting some shut-eye. I consulted the sloth panel to see if they had any advice for humans who wanted to sleep as well as they do. Just thinking about it made them very drowsy, but I managed to get some tips out of them in between dozes.

CALM YOUR MIND

Switching off your internal monologue and relaxing is the most important part of sloth living. Nowhere is a racing internal monologue more apparent than when you're trying to sleep. A slothful breathing exercise could help.

You're already lying down, so you should be able to adopt the downward-facing sloth position pretty easily, but however you choose to lie, fix all your attention on your breathing. Trace the air as it enters your nostrils, travels down your throat and enters your lungs. Then follow the air again as it leaves your body.

Thoughts will float through your mind, but try not to let them distract you from the exercise. Bring your mind back to your breathing every time it races away.

Try not to worry about what you did today, or what you have to do tomorrow. Just focus on the present like a sloth on an especially comfy branch who's about to drift into a deep sleep.

It takes a lot of practice to master breathing exercises, and it's easy to get frustrated and feel like they're not working. But stick to them with the patience and determination of the sloth, and they should eventually work.

CUT BACK ON CAFFEINE

You'd never catch a sloth asking for a venti skinny caramel macchiato with cream. For a start, the coffee shop would be closed before it got through the question.

Sloths don't bother drinking much at all, but they get plenty of water from leaves. Try cutting back on coffee, tea and soft drinks with caffeine, or cut them out altogether. At least then you won't be that person in the coffee shop nursing their fifth flat white of the afternoon while saying they struggle to sleep and they have no idea why.

STICK TO A SLEEP PATTERN

Sloths love to nap, and will even nod off right in the middle of an especially exciting branch. For humans, on the other hand, this can be a bad idea. If you're having problems with sleep, it can be tempting to take it when you can get it. But it's better to stick to a pattern. Wake up at the same time every day, even if it's the weekend and you've got a chance to make up the four hours last night you spent alternating between feeling too hot with your duvet on and too cold without it.

Your bed might start to look very welcoming at two in the afternoon, but napping in the day can disturb your sleep at night. Stick to a routine and let your mind associate sleep with darkness.

EXERCISE

Sloths might be ready for a doze after just shuffling along a branch for a while, but humans need to earn tiredness. Try going for a long, slothful walk in the park at lunchtime and see if it helps you sleep better at night.

ASSOCIATE YOUR BED WITH SLEEP

Doing too many different things in bed can make it harder to sleep there. I don't mean 'different things in bed' in the glossy magazine sense, by the way. If that's the reason you're missing out on sleep, you probably won't mind too much.

I mean things like propping your laptop on a pillow to get a little extra work done in the evenings, or checking your emails on a tablet before you go to sleep.

Sloths might get away with using the same branch for napping, eating and the urgent business of staring at the sky, but you might find it easier to nod off if you use your bed purely for sleeping.

HIDE YOUR CLOCKS

Sloths don't have the harsh light of a radio alarm clock shining into their eyes as they try to sleep. Is it any wonder they're so good at dozing off?

Bedside clocks are a terrible idea for those who have trouble sleeping. It's incredibly difficult to resist peeking at them to check if the time you've spent tossing and turning has really been three hours, or if it was actually just a few minutes. Every time you glance at a clock, it gives you a fresh shot of worry about how little sleep you're getting and how you're going to be a drooling zombie the next day.

Move your bedside clock and watch into a distant drawer so you won't be tempted to look at them. And the same goes for your phone, of course. The last thing you want to do is post on Facebook about how you're having trouble sleeping, and get into a chat with fellow insomniacs that keeps you awake until morning.

DON'T EAT TOO CLOSE TO BEDTIME

Sloths may be able to fall asleep pretty much mid-munch, but humans should give their digestive system a chance to do its stuff before bedtime. Sloths only have to digest a few leaves, but if you eat a late supper of obscure cheeses, fried chicken and prawn vindaloo, don't be surprised if your stomach keeps you awake to let you know how hard it's working.

COUNT SLOTHS

Instead of counting imaginary sheep as they jump over a fence, picture sloths approaching the fence at their natural pace, scaling it and crawling away on the other side. By the time you've got to ten, you'll either be asleep or it will be morning.

PICTURE YOURSELF AS A SLOTH

Visualizing yourself in a relaxing place has been shown to help sleep. Thinking about the specific details of a scene can distract you from your thoughts long enough to let you drift off. The usual suggestions are beaches and meadows, but the technique will also work if you imagine yourself slouching on a branch in the middle of a rainforest.

Two-toed sloths actually have three toes. They only have two claws on their forelimbs, but they have three on their hind limbs. But they don't mind what anyone thinks of them, so they never bother to correct this.

CHAPTER 14

The Sloth Style Guide

In order to truly understand the sloth, you must become the sloth. And while having a small furry head that swivels through 270 degrees must remain an impossible dream for most of us, there are a few ways you can let the sloth guide your look.

CRUMPLED CLOTHES

Although the sloth would be excellent at ironing with its long limbs and firm grip, there's no way it would ever bother. Sloths would rather spend a few more minutes relaxing than ironing jeans, and so should you. Slightly crumpled clothes should be worn at all times by all slothfulness experts.

CAMOUFLAGE

Sloths escape predators by blending in with their natural environment and there's no reason you can't do the same. Buy a shirt that's the same colour as the wall you sit near, and go unnoticed by annoying colleagues.

BOWL CUT

The brown-throated sloth, which is found in the rainforests of South and Central America, has beige fur on its face, but darker hair on its head and forehead. As a result, it looks like its mum has stuck a bowl on its head, snipped around it and assured it that no one at school will notice it didn't go to a proper hairdresser. You may wish to give yourself a bowl cut as you master the art of slothfulness. It will prove to the world that you're confident enough not to worry what anyone thinks.

BIG HAIR

The maned sloth, which lives in Brazil, has long fur surrounding its face, giving it the look of an especially lazy seventies rocker. This can be a good alternative to the bowl cut for bold sloth lovers.

THE SAME CLOTHES EVERY DAY

Wearing the exact samo things for days on end might be taking things a bit far. Unlike the sloth, you have sweat glands, and your clothes will need washing eventually. But wearing similar clothes every day can bring a slothful simplicity to your life. You won't have to waste time deciding what to wear, and you can use the extra time to practise slothfulness.

LOOSE CLOTHES

You never know when you'll get the chance to do some sloth yoga, so make sure you're always wearing light, comfortable clothing. Avoid skinny jeans, tight shirts and heavy jackets if you want to practise the upward-grasping sloth in a spare moment.

COMFORTABLE SHOES

You'll find it easier to fit more slothful walking into your day if you're always wearing practical shoes. You should be able to focus your attention entirely on your surroundings while you walk, and shoes that pinch your feet or make you topple over won't help.

ODD SOCKS

Wearing socks that don't match is one of the great taboos of human society. You might as well walk around naked as with one red sock and one green one. And yet our socks push us to this fate by going missing one at a time until the only ones left are mismatched. Most people waste hours frantically hunting under beds and behind sofas when this happens. But the slothful human will simply accept it, pull on two odd socks, and enjoy the time they've saved.

SLEEVED BLANKETS

For the ultimate in slothful relaxation, try a blanket with sleeves. Now you can grab your mug without having to take your arms out from under your blanket. You know it's what sloths would choose if they didn't have all that lovely warm fur.

MOHAIR JUMPERS

Wearing a fluffy jumper that resembles the fur of the sloth can help to remind you of the creature you aspire to be. Alternate between a beige one and a green one for when you want to pretend you're covered in algae.

SLOTH ONESIES

After a few years of wearing all the other sloth style staples, you will finally be ready to graduate to the apex — the sloth onesie. Only the most relaxed and confident humans will have the courage to turn up for work dressed as a giant sloth, especially if they work in the army or police force. But it is only by wearing this furry one-piece garment that you can truly show the world you've reached sloth enlightenment.

Female sloths sometimes attempt to attract mates with high-pitched screams. It's not known why male sloths find this so attractive, or if the females are still in the mood by the time potential mates finally make it to her.

CHAPTER 15

Slothful Dating

The mating rituals of the sloth are mysterious, and experts don't know for sure what traits the creatures find attractive in each other. But female sloths sometimes let out a high screech that is thought to be a mating call. Male sloths head towards the source of the noise, though Miss Sloth will presumably be waiting a while.

In a further bizarre twist, female sloths upgrade their weekly poo to a daily one when they're on heat, which is thought to be a way of advertising their presence to males. This is unlikely to work in human dating.

Sloth sex doesn't take very long, and they don't tend to hang around much afterwards. They pretty much just pretend they'll keep in touch and lurch off home.

Sloths generally live alone, although a female and her offspring will stay close for up to four years.

All this might seem to be a bleak picture of coupling, and nothing to aspire to. But perhaps the attitude of sloths could be useful in the human dating game, even if the specifics of their behaviour aren't.

Approaching the search for a partner with a relaxed, sloth-like attitude can make the experience less stressful. And you might just find someone else who wants to live at 0.15 miles per hour.

Here are a few ways sloth living can help with the dating game.

DATE AT SLOTH SPEED

Just as the sloth is in no hurry to find the right tree, so you should be patient finding the right person. Like the sloth, you'll get there in the end. This doesn't mean you should reject an otherwise perfect partner because one of their earlobes is bigger than the other. But neither should you rush into it.

As with so many other aspects of life, comparisons can be unhelpful. You may have old friends aggressively racking up life milestones as if they were points in a computer game. One minute they're engaged, the next they're married, the next they're homeowners, the next they're parents.

Forcing yourself to keep pace with these people isn't going to end well. Just remember the sloth, making its way along the branch, unaware of what rival sloths are doing on other trees, but content with its own progress.

And the sloth pace can continue even when you've found someone. Leave time between messages, suggest meeting up next week rather than tomorrow, and don't feel the need to overshare right at the start. Revealing too much about yourself straight away can make someone feel uncomfortable, especially if you're giving details about previous relationships. There will be plenty of time for that later on, but stick to sloth pace at first.

GET INTO A SLOTHFUL STATE BEFORE A DATE

Try performing a slothfulness exercise before a date, such as focusing on your breathing. It could help you relax, and approach your date in an open frame of mind.

It's easy to fit every experience into the stories we tell about ourselves, whether it's that certain types of people are wrong for us, or that we've been damaged by a previous relationship. Try to free yourself from these thoughts so you can engage with the present.

SUGGEST A SLOTHFUL DATE

Find out what the slowest restaurant in your area is, and suggest it. How does your date react? If they keep tutting and snapping their fingers at the staff, the chances are they're not good sloth material.

Even in a well-staffed and efficient restaurant, you can test your date by taking a long time to decide. Then choose a salad and savour the leaves at a sloth-like pace to see if they keep looking at their watch. But try not to get so tuned into the sloth mindset that you eat the flowers from the middle of the table. Your date might remember that they have an important appointment they've forgotten about.

If things develop, suggest long walks and relaxing nights in.

If your date rejects these in favour of playing squash or riding roller coasters, it could be another sign that they won't suit sloth living.

LISTEN

Developing sloth-like patience and learning to focus on the present can make you a good listener, which is a surprisingly rare skill. It means you can concentrate on what someone's saying and ask relevant questions instead of launching into a monologue on a vaguely related topic.

PROJECT SLOTH CONFIDENCE

Sloths are happy to be themselves, so take inspiration from them. Trying to present an idealized version of yourself will waste your energy and prevent honest engagement. Look at the sloth. It never gets a haircut and it spends months covered in algae, yet it's adorable.

RETURN TO YOUR SLOTHFUL STATE AFTER A DATE

Just as going into a date with an open mind is important, so it can be useful to be aware of your thoughts afterwards. Take another few moments to concentrate on your breathing and observe your inner monologue.

KNOW WHEN TO SWITCH OUT OF SLOTH MODE

Useful though the sloth approach might be, there will come a time when you know someone isn't right. If your date mentions their love of Adam Sandler comedies or alt-right websites, it's time to switch from sloth mode to cheetah mode and get out of there.

This is why it's sometimes better to arrange a lunchtime meet-up before going on a full evening date. It's much easier to pretend you've been called back into the office at one in the afternoon than nine at night.

CHAPTER 16

The Slothful Parent

You might think that parenthood is the time in your life when slothful behaviour would be least useful. It's no use relaxing in the downward-facing sloth position if you have a toddler jumping on your back and covering you with *Paw Patrol* stickers. Yet even in these hectic times the sloth can be a good role model.

Although sloths are generally solitary creatures, they make an exception for parenting. Baby sloths cling to their mothers for a few weeks after they're born. They stay at their mother's side for up to four years before slouching off for a life of their own. As sloths don't have any dirty laundry to bring back at weekends, that's pretty much it.

The human's relationship with its infant is much more complicated, and goes on for even longer than four years. But the wisdom of the sloth can help.

BABIES

Human babies might not be quite as cute as sloth ones, but they come pretty close. And while they don't attach themselves to you for weeks at a time, you might still struggle to get a moment to yourself to practise slothfulness.

And even if you do grab some time, things might not go according to plan. A simple breathing exercise can soon turn into a snoring one as you keel over and make up some of the hundreds of hours of sleep you've missed.

But there are ways to find time for slothful calm while looking after your baby. Parts of your childcare routine such as bathing, feeding and pushing in the buggy can be transformed into slothfulness exercises. Probably not nappy changing, though. That's never going to be relaxing.

Concentrate on the physical sensations of these things and bring your attention to the present moment. The early part of parenthood is pretty overwhelming, and you'll find worry, frustration and joy whizzing around your mind. Notice your thoughts, but don't dwell on them. Keep bringing your attention back to the simple task you're doing.

TODDLERS

Now your child can move around, you can add physical exhaustion to the sleeplessness and worry. You might not feel much like a sloth as you run around after your child and ask them to stop eating crayons, but the principles of slothfulness can guide you through the madness.

The slothful parent embraces the imperfections of life with a toddler. Cups will break, walls will be drawn on and you'll leave the house with a stain on your T-shirt that you pray is milk and not puke. Your minimalist living space will be swamped with Duplo and your one moment of peace will be shattered as you accidentally step on that toy fire truck with the really loud siren.

Using the evenings for slothfulness exercises is important, even if you find yourself flopping over and going to sleep three seconds in. There will be times when you need to draw on the calmness the following day, like when your toddler is crying, shouting and stamping their feet, or when you're about to do the same.

Make the most of the moments of calm during the day too. Your child might be glugging milk, drawing a picture or playing with a toy, giving you a chance to focus on relaxing.

OLDER CHILDREN

As your children get older, you might find that all their waking hours are filled with hectic activities. When they're not at school, they're in after-school clubs, and when they're not frantically trying to get their homework done, they're trying to complete a computer game.

Even the most energetic child will get run down by all this eventually. As well as making space in your own life for sloth-like peace, try to do the same for theirs. Set time aside for quieter activities you can do together like painting or rural walks. And encouraging them to read instead of gazing at screens can introduce some much-needed calm into their lives.

TEENS

You might think your children have already turned into sloths when they hit puberty. They become lie-in experts and quite possibly have algae growing all over them. If it weren't for their permanent frowns it would be hard to tell them apart.

In truth, the teenage years aren't very slothful at all. The emotional state of many teens couldn't be further from sloth-like tranquillity. As they strive to establish their identity, everything can turn into an exhausting battle of wills.

In these times your slothfulness will be tested to the full. Try to channel the calm of the sloth and take time to really listen to them. Avoid turning every conversation into an opportunity to dispense parental wisdom. Even if what you're saying is reasonable, it can come across like you're shutting discussion down.

Listen to your teen, and take time to understand the points they're making. They might not always be consistent, but this is to be expected when they're forming their identity.

At some times, conflict will be inevitable. Your teenager is finding out who they are through argument and opposition. If this happens, at least make sure you put time aside for slothful calm on your own.

CHAPTER 17

The Sloth Guide to Modern Irritations

Throughout this book, our wise sloth panel has advised on the important aspects of human life. But there are many more trivial aspects of existence that can push us over the edge unless we seek out slothful calm. Here's a selection of modern irritations and what to do about them.

CAR ALARMS

We've all been there. A car alarm wakes you up in the middle of the night and you immediately rush out, valuing your neighbour's property more than your own life. Or rather, you shove your fingers in your ears and grind your teeth. And your neighbour does the same because they think it's your alarm because they all sound the same.

The sloths had a lot of sympathy with this problem. They say that sometimes the mating calls of local birds such as the bare-throated bellbird and the screaming piha are so loud that their pleasant dozes are interrupted. But if the noise wakes you up, it can be your angry reaction that keeps you awake. They recommend getting into the downward-facing sloth position and concentrating on your breathing in an effort to escape your thoughts until drowsiness takes hold.

PASSWORDS

All you want to do is buy a pair of shoes, or book tickets to a local theatre, but the website won't let you check out without registering. And it won't let you register without devising a password so complicated that only a quantum physicist would be able to look at it without going insane. You know you won't remember it, but you go ahead anyway, a slave to the demands of the jumped-up site.

The initial advice from the sloths was to abandon the online purchase and go outside and grab a twig for free instead. But when I suggested that the problem might occur if you were buying something important like a yoga mat or sloth onesie, they gave it some more thought. The sloths concluded that you might as well write your passwords on a piece of paper and keep it next to your computer. It's possible that someone might break into your house and order extra shoes for you with the stolen information, but it's certain that you'll forget it if you don't.

TELEMARKETING CALLS

You jump out of the bath to take an important call, only to hear someone asking if you were involved in an accident you didn't get compensation for. You yell that you weren't, but they will be if they ever call again. Then you feel terrible for shouting at someone who's just trying to make ends meet and you wonder what your old radical student self would have made of your behaviour.

The sloths said they would never disturb a swim for anyone, no matter how loudly they shouted. They said that humans should remember to turn off all digital distractions including their phones before periods of slothful relaxation such as baths.

READING THE COMMENTS

You've just finished watching a delightful YouTube video of a startled kitten, and you decide to glance down at the comments. You expect to see 'OMG THAT IS SO CUTE' followed by a love heart emoji. What you find instead is that it's somehow inspired an angry debate between a right-wing troll and an easily goaded liberal.

Our panel advise staying away from the internet altogether, except for vital things like online banking and baby sloth videos. But if you insist on surfing the web, as people from the nineties call it, stay the hell away from the comments.

SITTING NEXT TO THAT LOUD GUY ON THE TRAIN

For once, you've found a seat on a train. And even better, it's one with a table. The man opposite seems harmless enough, so it's time to sit back, gaze at the passing trees and slip into a state of slothful bliss. Then the man makes a call. He's yelling so loudly you wonder if he really needs the phone at all. Surely Ian from finance can hear him from the train?

Then he makes another call. Then another. None of them seem so urgent that he couldn't have emailed instead.

You start to wonder if the loud guy only makes these calls in public because he likes sounding important.

As with the car alarm, the sloths feel our pain. There are many times when their peaceful moments are interrupted by a howler monkey leaping onto their branch and letting out horrid guttural growls. They apparently do it to protect their territory, so not that different from train guy really.

And much like the car alarm, the answer could be to try a slothfulness exercise and lull yourself into a state of tranquillity that even train guy can't ruin. Either that or make the cry of the howler monkey until he realizes the carriage is your territory and goes away.

SPOILERS

You've been looking forward to the conclusion to your favourite TV show for weeks. But you wake up on the day of the series finale to find that some vague social-media acquaintance has already watched it and revealed the twist ending.

Our sloth panel had little sympathy for this one. They couldn't understand why anyone would want to watch TV instead of clouds in the first place. One of the sloths mentioned that a bird on a higher branch once described a cloud it couldn't see yet, which was a kind of spoiler. But it still enjoyed it anyway.

PASSIVE-AGGRESSIVE PEOPLE

The sloth is pretty clear about which of its neighbours are out to get it. They're either harmless, like the aye-aye, or deadly, like the harpy eagle. What the sloth doesn't have to reckon with is anything that pretends to be innocuous while secretly planning to rip you apart with its talons.

Things aren't so simple for humans. People might say things which are outwardly polite, but are actually quite insulting when you think about them later. They might write a note about how it would be great if everyone could wash their cups straight after using them and title it 'polite notice'. They can lace every compliment with an insult that cancels it out, like 'I'm so glad you were able to make it on Friday and it's such a shame you didn't feel like staying longer.' And any apology you get out of them will imply that the real fault was yours for overreacting.

The sloth panel agreed that this was very annoying behaviour, but reckoned ignoring it was probably the best option. Passive-aggressive people are sometimes just looking for a reaction and may give up if they don't get one.

At any rate, you ought to develop a greater sense of peace as you continue your journey into slothfulness. You'll accept that difficult people have their own issues, and you'll become harder to offend.

TIME-SAVING DEVICES THAT DON'T SAVE TIME

We once thought that technology would turn our lives into a paradise of endless leisure. We thought the biggest problem we'd face in the future would be deciding what to do with all the free time. Well, now we're in the future, and the free time doesn't seem to have shown up.

Part of the problem is that when things get easier, we decide they must be done more often. Using a washing machine is easier than beating your clothes against a rock next to a stream, so we decided that clothes need to be washed after just one wear. And that's even if we haven't spilled soup on them.

Sending emails is quicker than writing letters, so we make ourselves send five emails instead of one, and check our inboxes thousands of times more than we used to check our letter boxes. Underneath it all runs the ingrained idea that work is good and idleness is a sin.

The sloth panel said they had no interest in any technology, but if humans insist on using it they should at least take advantage of the extra time it gives them. Next time you're using the vacuum cleaner or the dishwasher, think about the time you've saved and use it for slothful relaxation instead of more chores.

MANSPLAINING

Mansplaining occurs when a human male describes something in a patronizing way to a human female. It helps if the human female has a PhD in the subject, while the human male has only skimmed the Wikipedia page.

Male and female sloths don't usually bother communicating, except during mating, when they're too busy with sloth loving to chat. But the sloths said they can sympathize, because they're sick of people like David Attenborough wading into the rainforest and humansplaining to them.

The sloths said that while it's usually better to let insults go, you should confront mansplainers. These people aren't deliberately trying to be rude, they have simply assumed they know more than you. Don't miss the chance to set them straight, and while you're at it, tell them what mansplaining is in the most condescending terms possible.

NOISY PEOPLE IN THE CINEMA

They come in late. They whisper. They talk. They ask stupid questions which they'd know the answer to if they were concentrating instead of talking. The gaze at glowing phones. They guess the ending. They chew. They slurp. They rustle. They sniff. They cough. And all while sitting right in front of you with gigantic hats on.

You want to say something, but then you'll spend the rest of the film feeling bad about getting angry. So you sit there listening to the noisy people instead of the film.

The sloths weren't too sympathetic. They thought that films were too intense and frantic even if you don't have someone annoying near you. I described the plots of the greatest films ever made to them, and they didn't like the sound of any of them.

Perhaps the answer is to seek out your nearest art-house and watch a slower, quieter film. You're much less likely to get disruptive people, and one of the other cinephiles will tut aggressively if anyone so much as breathes loudly.

PHONE TREES

Sloths love trees. Without them they wouldn't have leaves to snack on and branches to hang from. But the sloth panel were dismayed to find out that one of the most irritating things in the human world is called the 'phone tree'.

Phone trees are the automated caller systems that read out menus and ask us to press an option so we can be directed along a certain branch. And, like the sloth, we're likely to be left dangling for hours.

You're already pretty annoyed by the time you're on the phone tree, because it took you half an hour to find the company's phone number on their website. You couldn't find anything that matched your query in the FAQs, so it's unlikely that a robotic receptionist is going to be able to help. But you struggle on, tackling the tree over and over again like a sloth with sticky claws.

The sloths agreed that this sounded like a very annoying experience. But as with queuing, they suggested managing your expectations. Take a few moments to perform a slothful breathing exercise, then settle down in a comfy chair and let your epic ascent of the phone tree begin.

Sloths conserve their energy for the important things in life like finding delicious leaves. Try to save your energy for the things that are most important to you.

Conclusion

I hope this book has inspired you to slow down to sloth pace. If it took you longer to finish than *The Lord of the Rings*, then it probably did.

Let the wisdom of the sloth guide you in every area of life:

Visit calming green spaces

Walk instead of driving

Eat leafy salads instead of fast food

Slow down to speed up at work

Declutter your living space

Carry out tasks at half speed

Save your energy for the things that mean most

Leave space in your day

Read books instead of work emails at home

Do one thing at a time, and give it your full concentration

Switching to sloth pace might not always be possible. If you're rushing to make a flight, slowing down to 0.15 miles per hour might not be the best decision. But no matter how hectic things get, you should always set aside time to channel the sloth.

Picture the majestic creature as it slowly makes its way along a branch in search of the perfect leaf, and soon the stresses of modern life will fall away, and you'll find yourself in a sloth-like state of bliss.

Anything in your daily routine can be transformed into a calming slothfulness exercise if you do it slowly and give it your full attention. Brushing your teeth, chopping vegetables, making the bed – these things can all be used as ways to introduce calm moments into your day.